PEGASUS ENCYCLOPEDIA LIBRARY

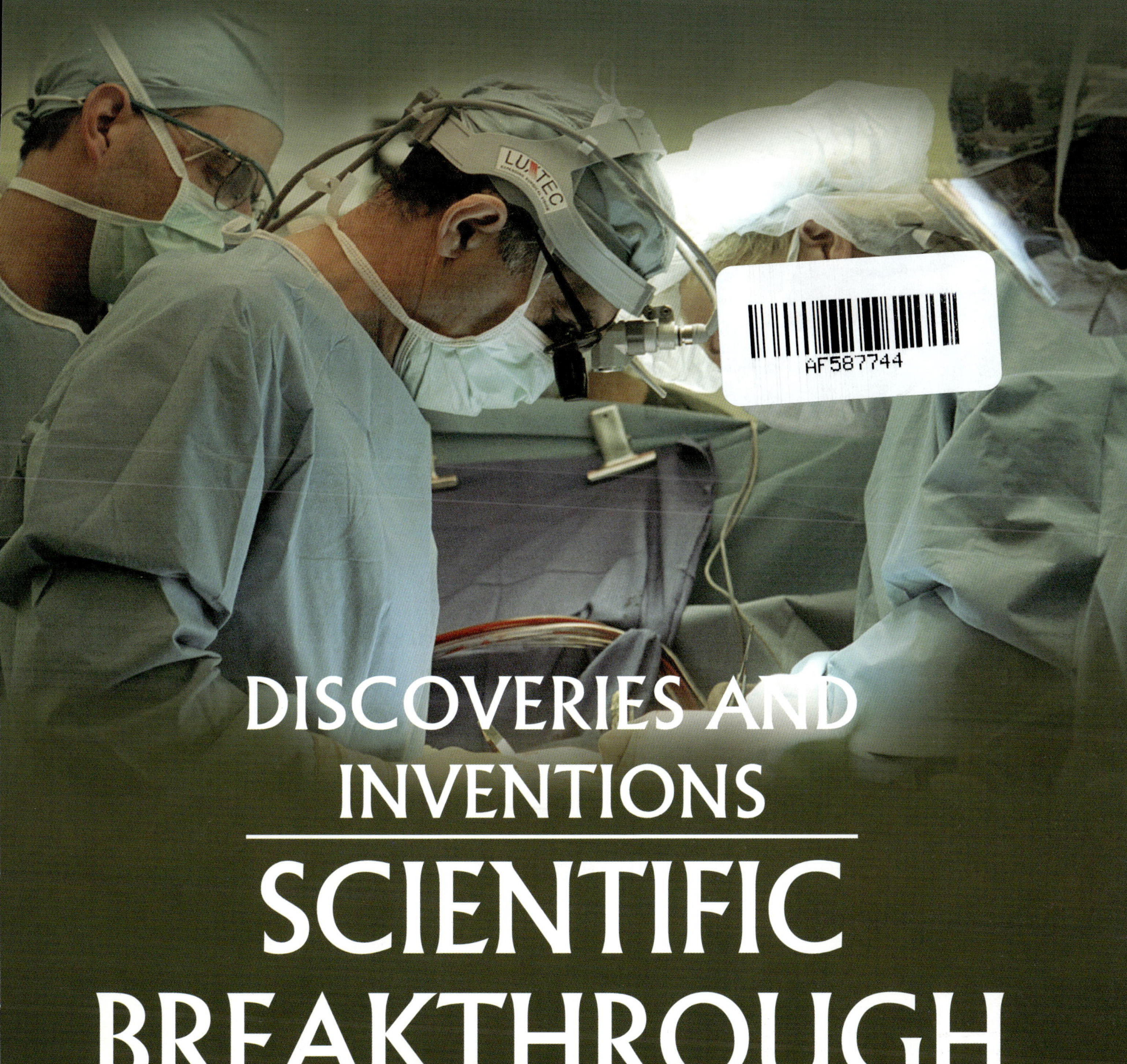




# DISCOVERIES AND INVENTIONS

# SCIENTIFIC BREAKTHROUGH

Edited by: Anil Kumar Tomar, Pallabi B. Tomar
Managing editor: Tapasi De
Designed by: Vijesh Chahal, Anil Kumar, Rohit Kumar
Illustrated by: Suman S. Roy, Tanoy Choudhury
Colouring done by: Vinay Kumar, Sonu, Kiran Kumari & Pradeep Kumar

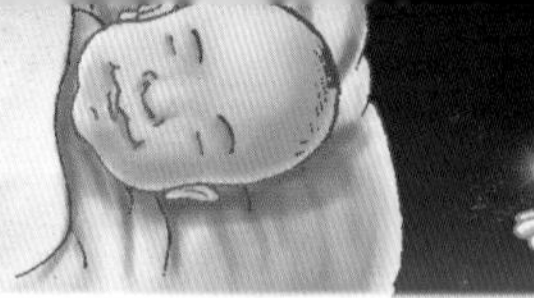

# CONTENTS

# The first heart transplant

South African cardiac surgeon, Dr Christiaan Barnard, is famous for performing the world's first successful human heart transplant.

Barnard was born on November 8, 1922, in Beaufort West, South Africa, son of a minister in Reformed Church. One of his brothers died of a heart problem while a toddler— an event which affected the Barnard family seriously.

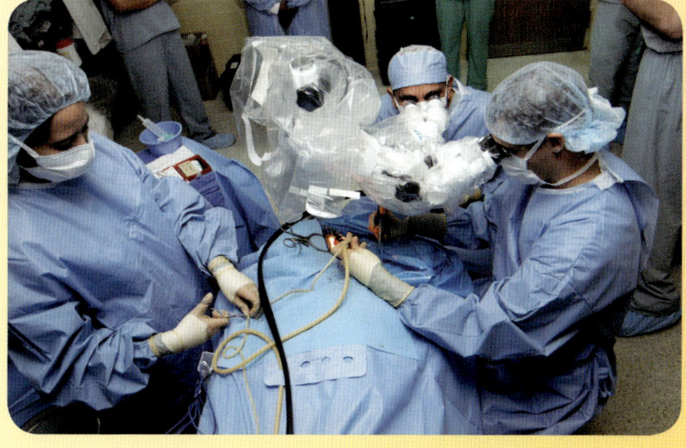

Barnard studied at the University of Cape Town Medical School, did his internship and residency at the Groote Schuur Hospital in Cape Town and became a general practitioner in Ceres, in Western Cape province.

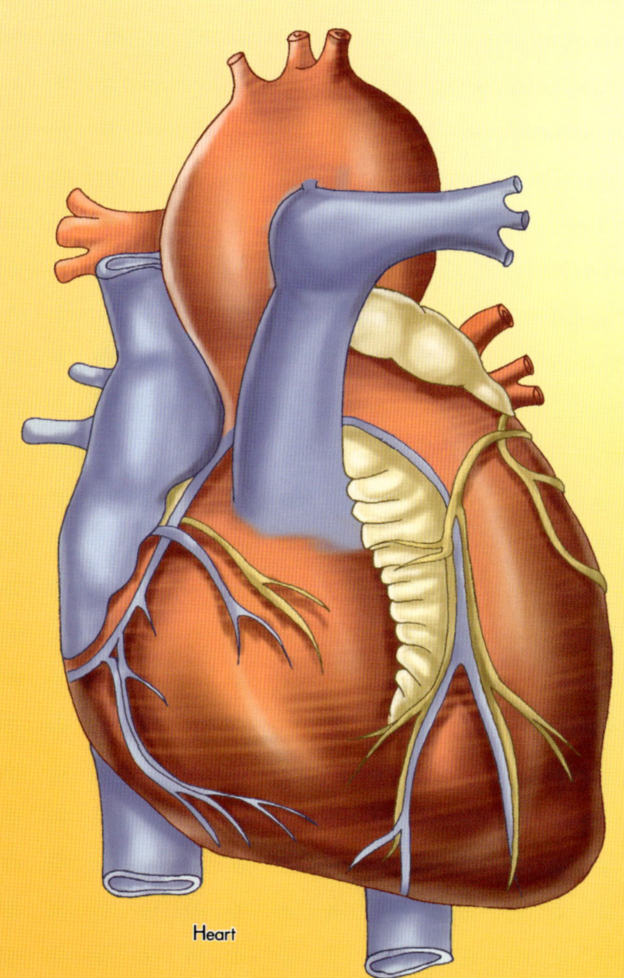

Heart

Barnard performed the world's first human heart transplant operation on 3 December, 1967 assisted by his brother, Marius Barnard, lasting nine hours and using a team of 30 persons.

The patient, Louis Washkansky was 55 years old and suffering from diabetes and heart disease. The transplant heart came from a young woman, Denise Darvall, killed in a road accident. Washkansky survived the operation and lived for 18 days, succumbing to pneumonia induced by the immuno-suppressive drugs he was taking.

**The first truly synthetic plastic was invented by Leo Baekeland, a Belgium chemist living in New York.**

# The first lunar landing

The first object from Earth to ever land on the Moon was the Soviet spacecraft Luna-2. It didn't land, but actually crashed into the Moon on September 14, 1959. It impacted the lunar surface west of Mare Serenitatis near the craters Aristides, Archimedes and Autolycus of the moon. Luna 2's mission was to help confirm the discovery of the solar wind turned up by Luna 1.

The first US spacecraft to impact the Moon was Ranger 7, which crashed into the Moon on July 31, 1964. This came after a string of failures with previous spacecraft in the Pioneer and Ranger line of robotic spacecraft.

The first spacecraft to make a soft landing on the Moon was the Soviet Luna-9 on February 3, 1966. Luna-9 was equipped with an airbag system that allowed it to crash into the Moon travelling more than 50 km/hour. The first even softer landing was made by US with Surveyor 1. It touched down on the surface of the Moon on June 2, 1966.

# The first man on the moon

The 1st man on the moon was the Apollo 11 Commander Neil Armstrong, who made history on July 20, 1969.

The Apollo 11 mission consisted of Command Module Pilot Michael Collins, Lunar Module Pilot Buzz Aldrin and Commander Neil Armstrong. The mission launched atop a Saturn V rocket on July 16, 1969. After a 4 day journey from the Earth to the Moon, the lunar module detached from the command module and landed on the surface of the Moon in the southern Sea of Tranquility.

The crew remained inside the module for 6 and half hours, preparing to make their exit onto the lunar surface. And then Neil Armstrong descended the ladder from the lunar module and onto the lunar surface. Buzz Aldrin followed Armstrong, and the two remained on the surface of the Moon for 2.5 hours, taking photographs, collecting rocks, drilling samples and placing scientific experiments. They gathered up all their samples, packed them in the lunar module, and left some souvenirs on the surface of the Moon like an American flag, Apollo 1 mission patch and commemorative plaque. They launched again and returned to Earth on July 24.

Michael Collins

Buzz Aldrin

Neil Armstrong

Robert Hutchings Goddard was an American physicist and inventor who is known as the father of modern rocketry.

# The first space satellite

The space age began with the October 4, 1957 launch of the first Russian space satellite. Other Sputnik satellites and the first US Explorer satellite soon followed.

## Sputnik 1

The space age began with the October 4, 1957 launch of the first artificial space satellite, Sputnik 1. The name Sputnik comes from Russian for 'companion' or 'fellow traveller'.

Sputnik 1 was a very simple satellite. It was a highly polished aluminum sphere. Sputnik 1 was 22 inches in diameter and weighed 183 pounds. Radio antennas extended from the sphere.

The first Sputnik's only instrumentation was a battery powered radio transmitter and a thermometer. Sputnik sent radio telemetry back to Earth. It orbited Earth every 98 minutes and fell back to Earth on January 4, 1958. The importance of this first Sputnik was not the data or telemetry but the simple fact that a manmade object had been launched into the orbit!

## Sputnik 2

When they realized the impact of the first Sputnik, Soviet leaders asked for a larger satellite launch in time to celebrate the 40th anniversary of the Russian revolution. Sputnik 2 was designed and built very quickly. It launched less than a month later on November 3, 1957.

Sputnik 2 was considerably larger. The 1,120 pound satellite carried the first passenger into space. A dog Laika, travelled into space but soon died when the capsule overheated. The satellite however remained in the orbit a little over 6 months.

## Sputnik 3

The first attempt to launch Sputnik 3 on April 27, 1958 failed. Sputnik 3 was however successfully launched on May 15, 1958. The 1.5 ton satellite contained a scientific payload with scientific instruments for measuring the conditions in space.

**In the 1980s, Luc Montagnier and Robert Gallo both separately discovered the retro virus known as HIV (Human Immunodeficiency Virus). This was also identified as the cause of AIDS.**

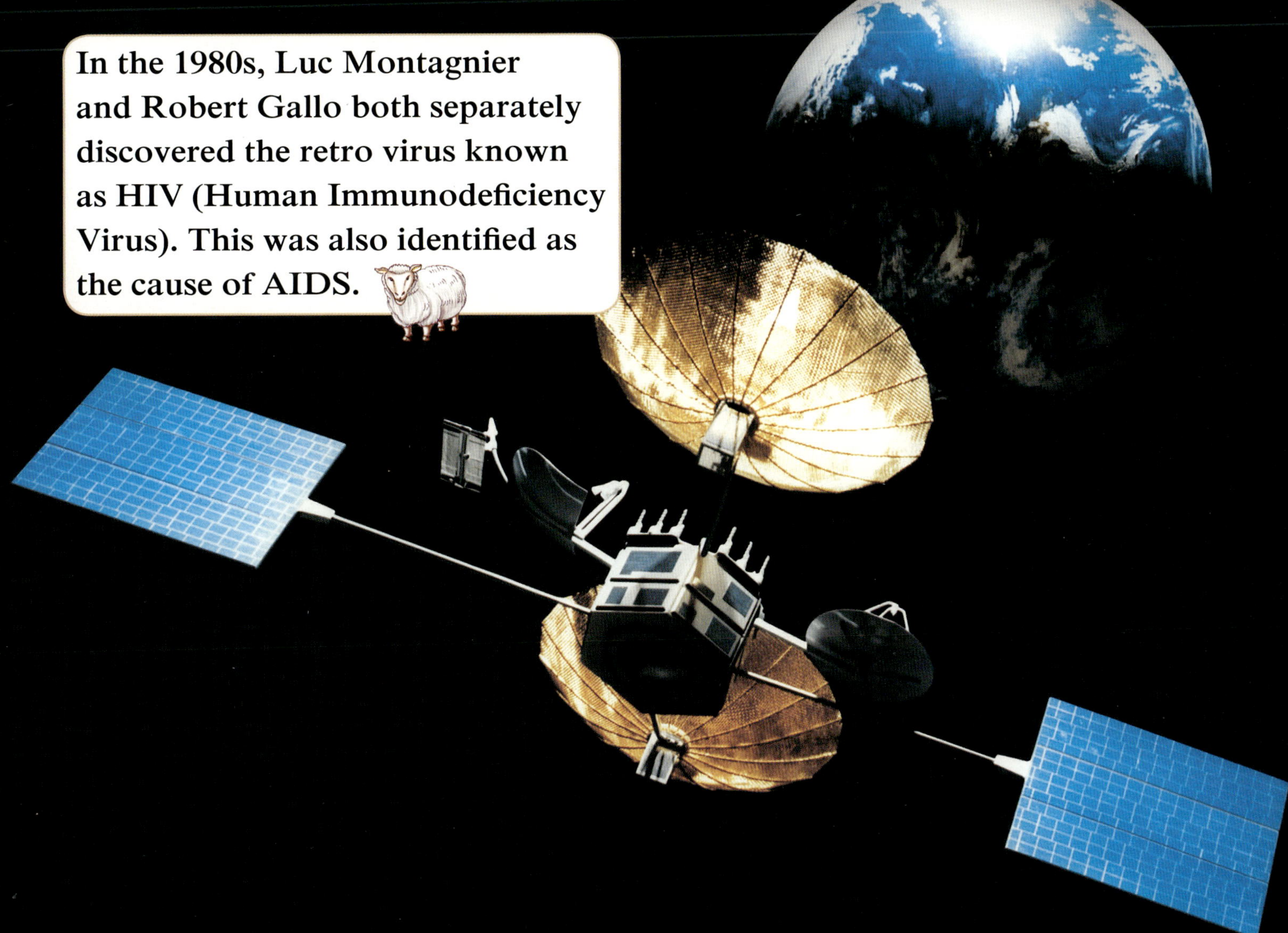

# The first photograph

Joseph Niepce

Niepce placed an engraving onto a metal plate coated in bitumen and then exposed it to light. The shadowy areas of the engraving blocked light, but the whiter areas permitted light to react with the chemicals on the plate. When Niepce placed the metal plate in a solvent, gradually an image, until then invisible, appeared. However, Niepce's photograph required eight hours of light exposure to be created and after appearing, would soon fade away.

A building photograph taken by Joseph Niepce in 1826 is known as the world's First Photograph but actually this is the earliest surviving photograph. This was captured by an eight-hour light exposure onto the plate to get the image. This over exposure resulted in sunlight on both sides of the building.

It represents the view of the courtyard of Niepce's house at Gras, France, taken from the window of his workroom. On the left side of the image is the pigeon-house and to the right of it is a pear-tree with a patch of sky showing through an opening in the branches. In the centre of the image is the slanting roof of the barn; the long building behind it is the bake house, with chimney. On the right side of the image is another wing of the house.

The first photographic image

**An 1909, Wilbur wright photographed the town of Centrocelli, Italy producing the first aerial photographs taken from an aeroplane.**

# Evolution of photography and its elements

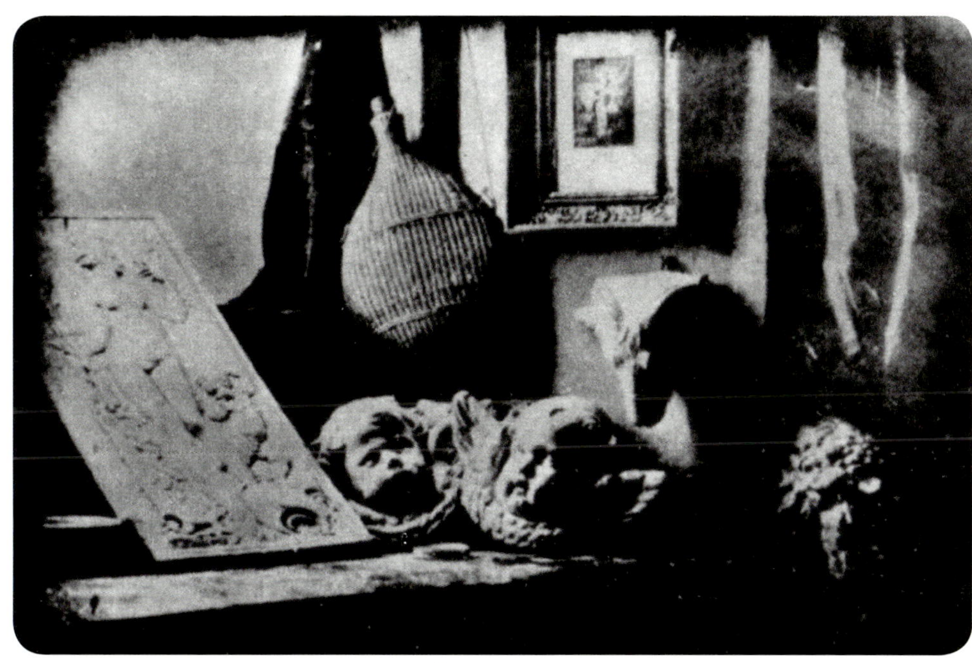

Daguerreotype

Archimedes, a prolific ancient Greek mathematician invented the water screw, a device for raising water using an encased screw open at both ends.

Louis Daguerre was the inventor of the first practical process of photography. In 1829, he formed a partnership with Niepce to improve the process he had developed.

In 1839 after several years of experimentation and Niepce's death, Daguerre developed a more convenient and effective method of photography, naming it after himself - **the daguerreotype**.

The inventor of the first negative from which multiple positive prints were made was Henry Fox Talbot, an English botanist and mathematician and a contemporary of Daguerre.

Talbot sensitized paper to light with a silver salt solution. He then exposed the paper to light. The background became black, and the subject was rendered in gradations of grey. This was a negative image, and from the paper negative, Talbot made contact prints, reversing the light and shadows to create a detailed picture. In 1841, he perfected this paper-negative process. The new process was called the calotype, from the Greek kalos, meaning 'beautiful'.

Tintypes, patented in 1856 by Hamilton Smith, were another medium that heralded the birth of photography. A thin sheet of iron was used to provide a base for light-sensitive material, yielding a positive image.

In 1851, Frederick Scoff Archer, an English sculptor, invented the wet plate negative. Using a viscous solution of collodion, he coated glass with light-sensitive silver salts. As it was glass and not paper, this wet plate created a more stable and detailed negative.

**Cellophane is a thin, transparent, waterproof protective film that is used in many types of packaging. It was invented in 1908 by Jacques Edwin Brandenberger, a Swiss chemist.**

Photography advanced considerably when sensitized materials could be coated on plate glass. However, wet plates had to be developed quickly before the emulsion dried. In the field, this meant carrying along a portable darkroom.

The first flexible roll films, dates back to 1889 were made of cellulose nitrate which is chemically similar to guncotton. A nitrate-based film deteriorates over time and releases harmful gases. It is also highly flammable. Thus, special storage for these types of films is required.

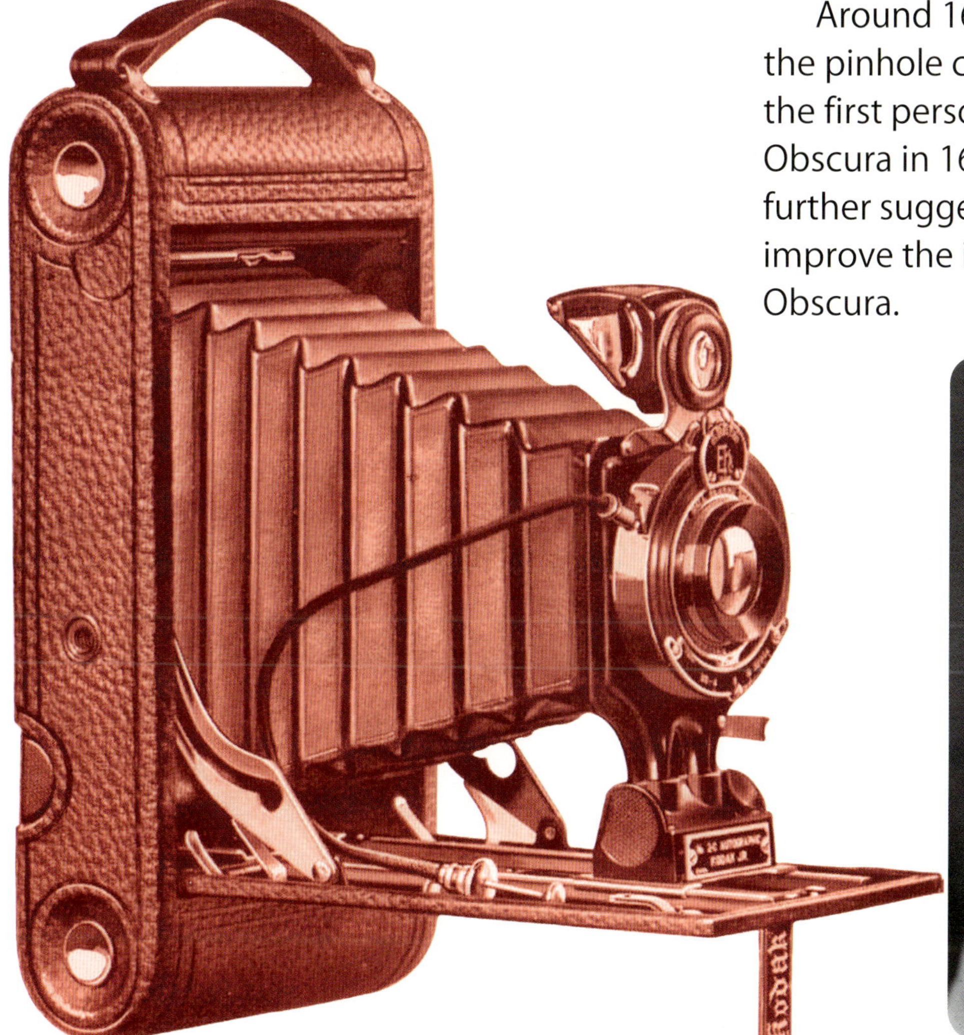

Around 1600, Della Porta reinvented the pinhole camera. Johannes Kepler was the first person to coin the phrase Camera Obscura in 1604, and in 1609, Kepler further suggested the use of a lens to improve the image projected by a Camera Obscura.

George Eastman

Nitrate film is historically important because it was used for the development of roll films. The first flexible movie film measured 35-mm wide and came in long rolls on a spool. In the mid-1920s, using this technology, 35-mm roll film was developed for the camera. By the late 1920s, medium-format roll film was created. It measured six centimetres wide and had a paper backing making it easy to handle in daylight. This led to the development of the twin-lens-reflex camera in 1929.

George Eastman, a dry plate manufacturer from Rochester, New York, invented the Kodak camera. For $22.00, an amateur could purchase a camera with enough film for 100 shots.

In 1879, the dry plate was invented, a glass negative plate with a dried gelatin emulsion. Dry plates could be stored for a period of time. Photographers no longer needed portable darkrooms and could now hire technicians to develop their photographs. Dry processes absorbed light so rapidly that the hand-held camera was now possible.

In 1889, George Eastman invented film with a base that was flexible, unbreakable and could be rolled. Emulsions coated on a cellulose nitrate film base, such as Eastman's, made the mass-produced box camera a reality.

Polaroid photography was invented by Edwin Herbert Land. Land was the American inventor and physicist whose one-step process for developing and printing photos created instant photography. The first Polaroid camera was sold to the public in November, 1948.

Edwin Herbert Land

Fuji introduced the disposable camera in 1986. In 1984, Canon demonstrated the first digital electronic still camera.

# The first test tube baby

On July 25, 1978, Louise Joy Brown, the world's first successful 'test-tube baby' was born in Great Britain. Though the technology that made her conception possible was heralded as a triumph in medicine and science, many feared that it would be ill-used in future.

Brown was born to Lesley and John Brown, who had been trying to conceive for nine years, but without success because of Lesley's blocked fallopian tubes. On November 10, 1977, Lesley underwent in vitro fertilization (IVF) procedure. Dr. Steptoe took an egg from one of her ovaries and Dr Edwards mixed that egg with John's sperm into a special solution. The fertilized egg was successfully embedded into Lesley's uterus wall.

Louise Joy Brown was born at 11:47 p.m., through a planned caesarean section delivered by Dr. John Webster, an obstetrician and gynaecologist at Oldham General Hospital, Oldham. She weighed 2.608 kg at birth. Her younger sister, Natalie Brown, was also conceived through IVF, four years later, and became the world's fortieth IVF baby and the first one to give birth herself—naturally—in 1999.

**Anders Celsius (1701-1744) was a Swedish professor of astronomy who devised the Celsius thermometer.**

# The first cloned animal

Dolly was the first mammal cloned from the DNA of an adult animal. She was a Finn Dorset sheep born in 1996 and was hailed as a monumental scientific breakthrough when her birth was announced in early 1997. Scientists at Scotland's Roslin Institute used somatic cell nuclear transfer (SCNT), a reproductive cloning method, to produce the lamb, which carried the same nuclear DNA as the donor sheep (the cells were taken from the donor's udders). Dolly made headlines around the world and launched a public debate about the possibilities and ethics of cloning. Over the years, research groups around the world reported the cloning of mice, rats, cows, goats, rabbits, pigs, a horse, a mule and a dog.

In 2003 Dolly was put to sleep. Though she lived only about half the expected 10 to 12 years life span for a Finn Dorset sheep, scientists who conducted a post-mortem examination of her found that other than her ailments (arthritis and lung cancer), she appeared to be normal. The celebrity sheep was the mother of six lambs, which were brought into the world in the old-fashioned way.

# The first computer

A historian might tell you that the first computer was the abacus, which was invented in Asia about 5000 years ago. However, the first modern computer was actually invented during World War II when a team of scientists and engineers at the University of Pennsylvania invented a general-purpose electronic digital calculator known as ENIAC (Electronic Numerator, Integrator, Analyzer, and Computer).

It consisted of 18,000 vacuum tubes and it was capable of adding 5,000 ten-digit decimal numbers per second. It also contained 7,200 crystal diodes, 1,500 relays, 70,000 resistors, 10,000 capacitors and around 5 million hand-soldered joints. It weighed approximately 30 short tons, took up about 1800 square feet (167 $m^2$), and consumed 150 kW of power.

It was the first large-scale, electronic, digital computer capable of being reprogrammed so that it could solve a variety of computing problems. The ENIAC was originally designed to calculate artillery firing tables for the U.S. Army's Ballistics Research Laboratory. However, some of the first problems that were run on the ENIAC were related to the design of the hydrogen bomb. The ENIAC was definitely a revolutionary development, which at that time was far ahead of any other calculators.

# The first computer mouse

The computer mouse as we know it today was invented and developed by Douglas Englebart during the 60's and was patented on November 17, 1970. While creating the mouse, Douglas was working at the Stanford Research Institute and originally referred to the mouse as a 'X-Y Position Indicator for a Display System'. This mouse was first used with the Xerox Alto computer system in 1973. However, because of its lack of success the first widely used mouse is credited to being the mouse found on the Apple Lisa computer. Today, the mouse is found and used on every computer.

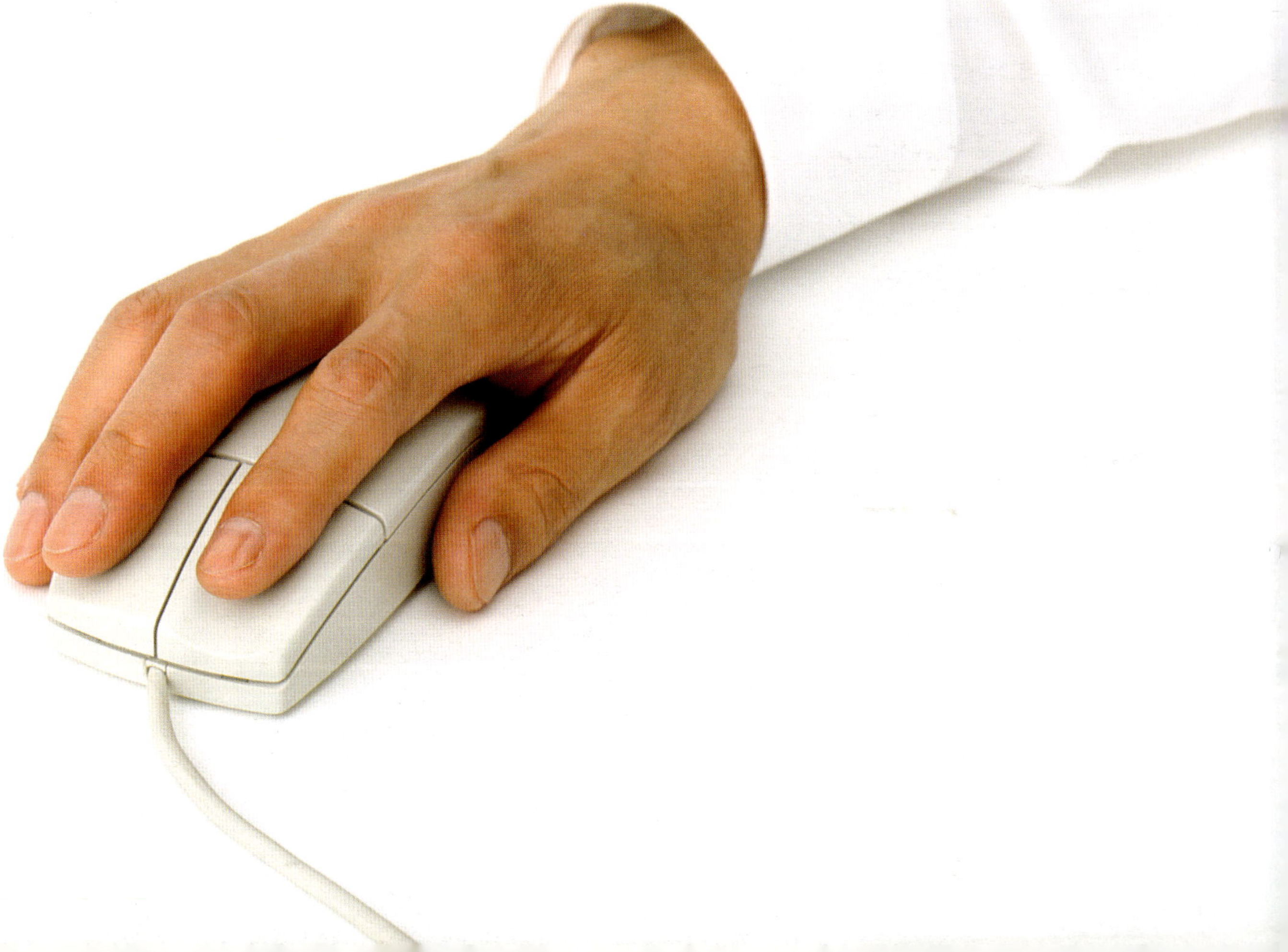

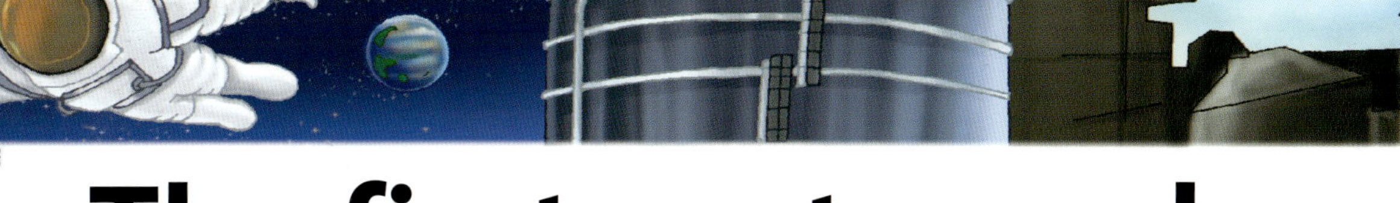



# The first motorcycle

American, Sylvester Howard Roper (1823-1896) invented a two-cylinder, steam-engine motorcycle (powered by coal) in 1867. This is considered as the first motorcycle.

A German called Gottlieb Daimler invented the first gas-engine motorcycle in 1885, which was an engine attached to a wooden bike. This invention marked the integration of the development of a viable gas-powered engine and the modern bicycle.

Gottlieb Daimler

Designed and built by the German inventors Gottlieb Daimler and Wilhelm Maybach in Bad Cannstatt (Stuttgart) in 1885, it was essentially a motorised bicycle. The inventors called their invention the **Reitwagen** ('riding car'). It was also the first petroleum-powered vehicle.

# The first X-Ray

Wilhelm Rontgen, a German physicist accidentally discovered X-rays when he was conducting experiments with the radiation from cathode rays. He noticed that the rays were able to penetrate opaque black paper wrapped around a cathode ray tube, causing a nearby table to glow with florescence. He also found that the new ray would pass through most substances casting shadows of solid objects on pieces of film. He named the new ray X-ray because in mathematics 'X' denotes the unknown quantity. Soon after he used a photographic plate and had his wife, Bertha, placed her hand in the path of the X-rays, creating the world's first X-ray picture. The news of Roentgen's discovery spread quickly throughout the world. In early 1896, X-rays began to be utilized clinically in the United States for capturing images of bone fractures and gunshot wounds. In 1901 Wilhelm Rontgen was awarded the very first Nobel Prize in Physics for this discovery.

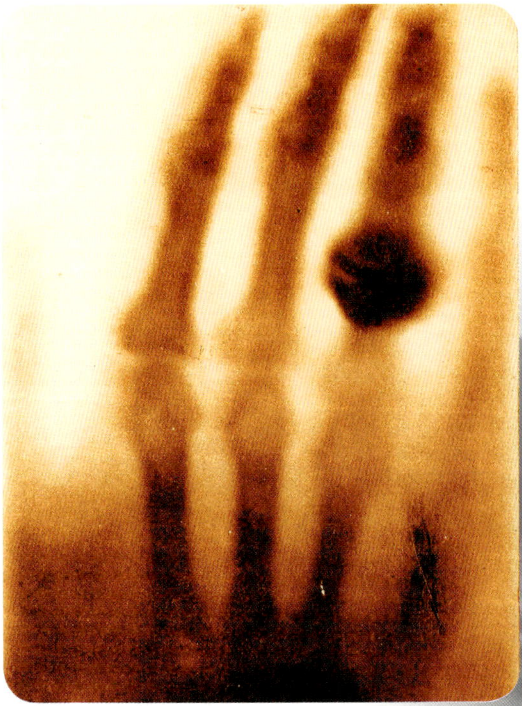

Wilhelm Rontgen

# The first microprocessor

A microprocessor, or a logic chip, is a computer processor on a microchip. It is an assembly of all the integrated circuits (ICs) to perform most of the functions of a computer's central processing unit (CPU).

In November, 1971, a company called Intel publicly introduced the world's first single chip microprocessor, the Intel 4004. It was invented by Intel engineers Federico Faggin, Ted Hoff, and Stan Mazor. After the invention of integrated circuits revolutionized computer design, the only place to go down was size of the processing unit. The Intel 4004 chip took the integrated circuit down one step further by placing all the parts that made a computer think (that is, central processing unit, memory, input and output controls) on one small chip. Programming intelligence into inanimate objects had now become possible.

**Lord Kelvin designed the Kelvin scale, in which 0 K is defined as absolute zero and the size of one degree is the same as the size of one degree Celsius.**

# Aspirin— the miracle drug

Gerhardt

Aspirin is so familiar that you don't even notice it in the medicine cabinet until you have a headache. Yet this little white pill was one of the first wonder drugs to be developed during modern times. Simple but surprisingly complex, researchers are still discovering the health-giving benefits of aspirin. First recorded in ancient Greece, a simple herbal remedy became a rock star in pharmacology around 1900.

The use of extracts made from the willow tree for pain management can be traced back to ancient times. The active ingredient in willow bark was extracted by Johann Buchner, in 1828, which he called salicin. In 1829, Henri Leroux extracted salicin in crystalline form for the first time. Raffaele Piria succeeded in obtaining the salicin in its pure state and called it 'salicylic acid'. The salicylic acid was tough on stomachs. This made scientists search for a means to neutralize it. The first person to do so was a French chemist, Charles Frederic Gerhardt. In 1853, Gerhardt neutralized salicylic acid by sodium and acetyl chloride, creating acetylsalicylic acid. Gerhardt's product was a great success but he abandoned his discovery as he had no desires to market it.

In 1899, Felix Hoffmann, rediscovered Gerhardt's formula. He gave it to his father who was suffering from the pain of arthritis. He found the drug very promising and convinced a German company called Bayer to market the new wonder drug. Aspirin was first sold as a powder and then, in 1915, the first Aspirin tablets were made.

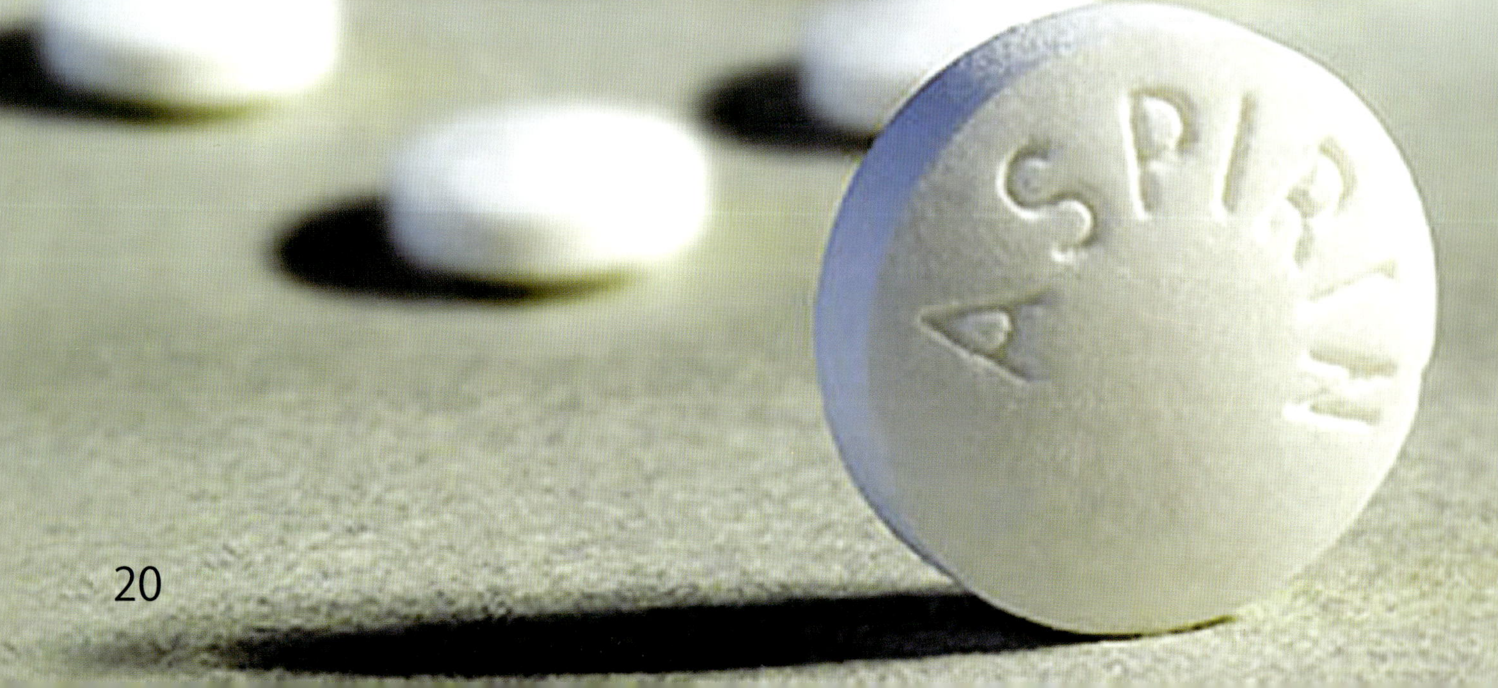

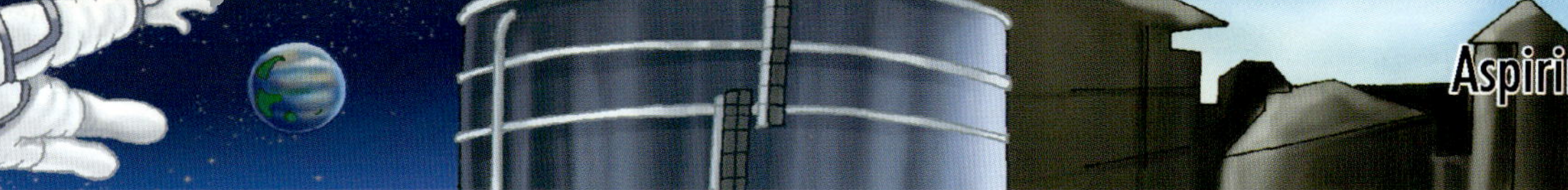

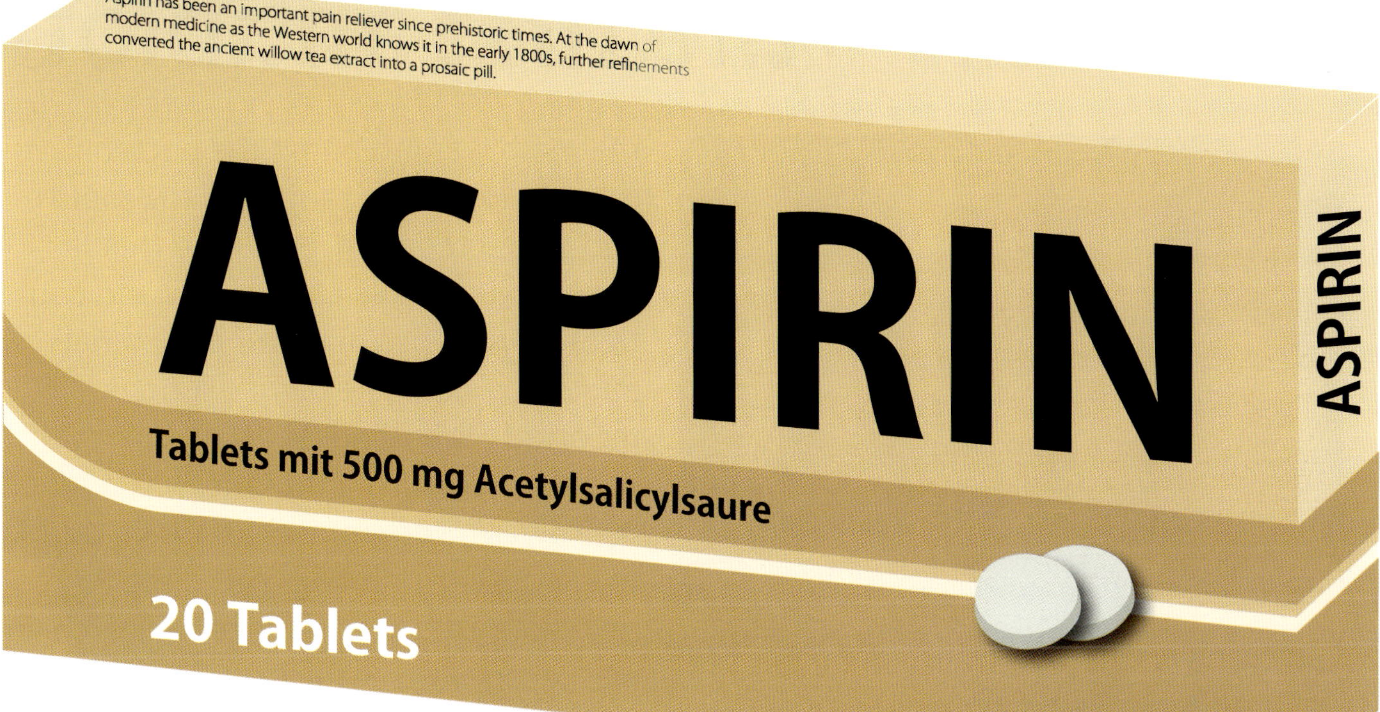


Aspirin has been an important pain reliever since prehistoric times. At the dawn of modern medicine as the Western world knows it in the early 1800s, further refinements converted the ancient willow tea extract into a prosaic pill. With the rise of international corporations in the early 1900s, the homely aspirin became a money maker for the German drug and dye giant Bayer.

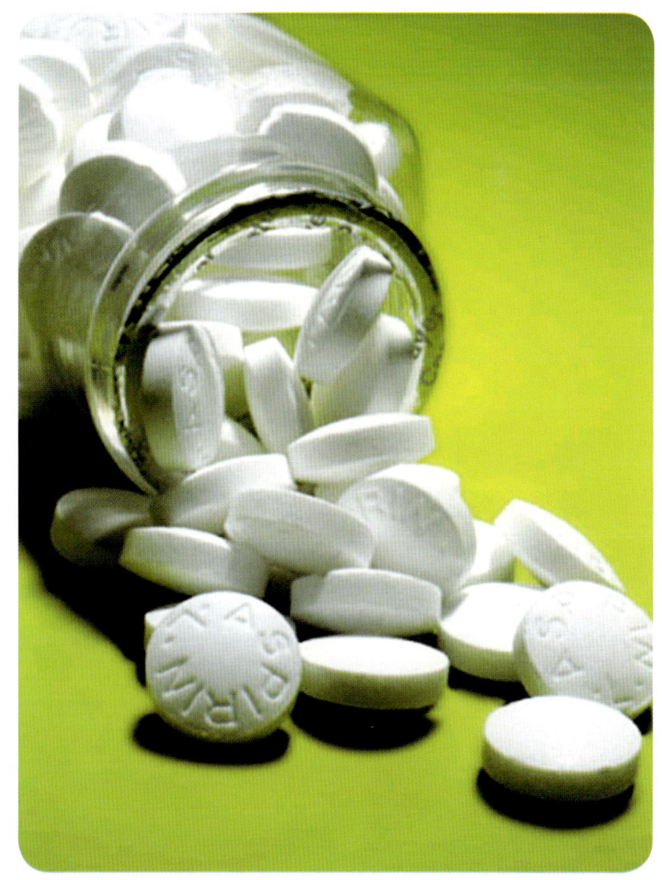

Aspirin has done miracles in the Spanish flu epidemic in 1918. It became extremely popular in the early part of the twentieth century. Generic version of Aspirin flooded American markets after Bayer's American patent of Aspirin expired in 1917. Aspirin continued to be the king of analgesics for half a century until it lost the war to advanced analgesics like paracetamol, which was introduced in 1956 and ibuprofen introduced in 1969.

# Penicillin—the first antibiotic

Alexander Fleming

Penicillin was discovered accidentally by Dr Alexander Fleming while working at St. Mary's Hospital in London. He was examining a culture of **Staphylococcus aureus**, a pathogenic bacterium when he noticed that it had been contaminated by a mold. He observed that species of the mold was inhibiting the bacterial growth. He took a sample of the mold and characterized it. He found that it belonged to penicillium family and could treat many types of harmful bacterial infections. Later, he named it penicillin and reported his findings in 1929. However, penicillin, the first antibiotic, was purified by Howard Florey and Ernst Chain during the Second World War. This discovery revolutionized the medicinal research and was recognized as the greatest advances in therapeutics. Fleming along with Florey and Chain received a Nobel Prize in 1945 for their discovery which led to the development of lifesaving antibiotics.

Ernst Chain

Howard Florey

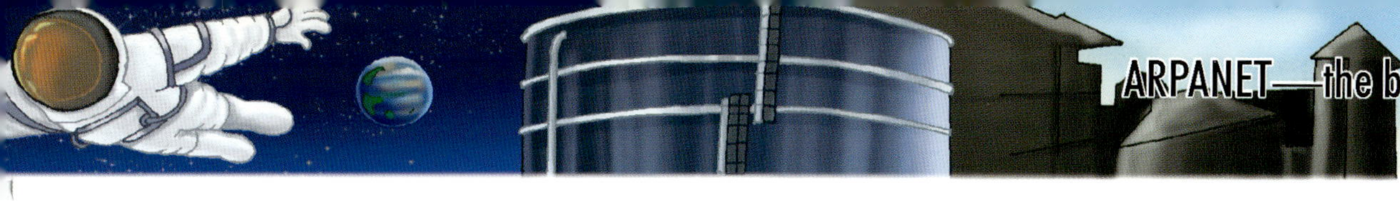

# ARPANET—the beginning of Internet

Internet is the network of networks which connects computer systems worldwide by various means such as telephone wires or satellites. The www (**World Wide Web**) is a network of sites that can be searched and retrieved by a special procedure known as a Hypertext Transfer protocol (HTTP). This protocol searches the address on the web servers and automatically retrieves the saved information for viewing.

The Internet technology was developed by Vinton Cerf in 1973 as part of a United States Department of Defense Advanced Research Projects Agency (DARPA) project. The computer network this project produced was called **ARPANET** that linked U.S. scientific and academic researchers.

ARPA scientists, working closely with experts in Stanford, developed a common language that would allow different networks to communicate with each other. This was known as a transmission control protocol/internet protocol (TCP/IP). Further developments in technology and World Wide Web, released the internet for everyone in 1991.

ADDRESS @ http://www.arpanet.

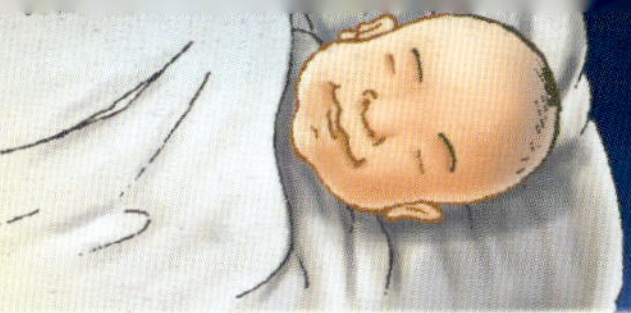

# Water purification

Humans have been storing and distributing water for centuries. The Greeks were among the first to gain an interest in water quality. They used aeration basins for water purification. The Romans were the first to construct water distribution networks in history. They used river, spring or groundwater for provisioning.

The first municipal water treatment plant for drinking water was built in Paisley, Scotland in 1804 by John Gibb, to supply drinking water to the entire city. This plant consisted of concentric sand and gravel filters, and its distribution system consisted of a horse and cart. In 1806, Paris operated a large water treatment plant where water was stored for 12 hours and filtered before supply. Filters consisted of sand and charcoal and were replaced every six hours.

In 1807, Glasgow, Scotland, was one of the first cities to pipe filtered water to consumers. By 1827, slow sand filters designed by Robert Thom were common in Scotland homes for drinking water purification. Similar systems were designed by James Simpson in London. Thom's filters were cleaned by backwash, while Simpson's required scraping. The Simpson design eventually became the famous English model throughout the world.

**Jean Bernard Léon Foucault, a French physicist, invented the gyroscope in 1852.**

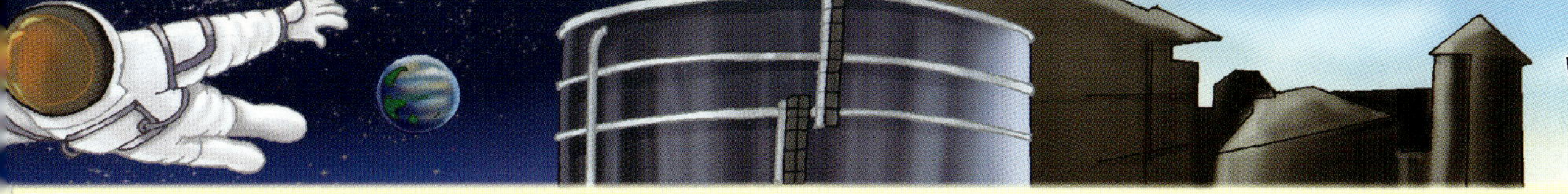



The drinking water, contaminated with microbes, can lead to a miserable bout of stomach pain and loose bowels, and a hasty trip to a local medical clinic. The World Health Organization reported that water borne diseases are the world's leading cause of death, claiming more number of deaths than the war, terrorism and weapons of mass destruction combined together. Children in impoverished countries, whose immune systems are weakened by malnutrition and other stresses, are particularly at higher risk. The condition used to be even worse in earlier times. For centuries, even in developed countries, mysterious periodic outbreaks of water-borne cholera regularly killed many thousands of people.

In 1854, British scientist John Snow found that the disease was caused by microorganisms in sewage that contaminated the water supply. He came up with the idea to add chlorine to the water. This practise successfully killed the microorganisms, and the illness rate plummeted. Since then, more chemical and filtration technologies have been developed to make our drinking water safe.

# Robot

A robot is generally a machine in the form of a human that can perform functions attributed to the humans. It is a reprogrammable, multifunctional manipulator designed to move material, parts, tools or specialized devices through various programmed motions for the performance of a variety of tasks. Karel Capek is credited for the first use of the word 'robot'.

In 1956, George C. Devol and Joseph F. Engelberger made a serious and commercially successful effort to develop a real, working robot. They persuaded Norman Schafler of Condec Corporation in Danbury that they had the basis of a commercial success. Engelberger started a manufacturing company 'Unimation' which stood for universal automation. In this way, the first commercial company to make robots was established. Their first robot was nicknamed the 'Unimate'. For his achievements in the field of robotics, Engelberger is known as the 'father of robotics'. The first Unimate robot was installed at the General Motors plant to work with heated die-casting machines. Most of the initial Unimates were sold to extract die castings and to perform spot welding on auto bodies, both tasks being particularly hateful jobs for people.

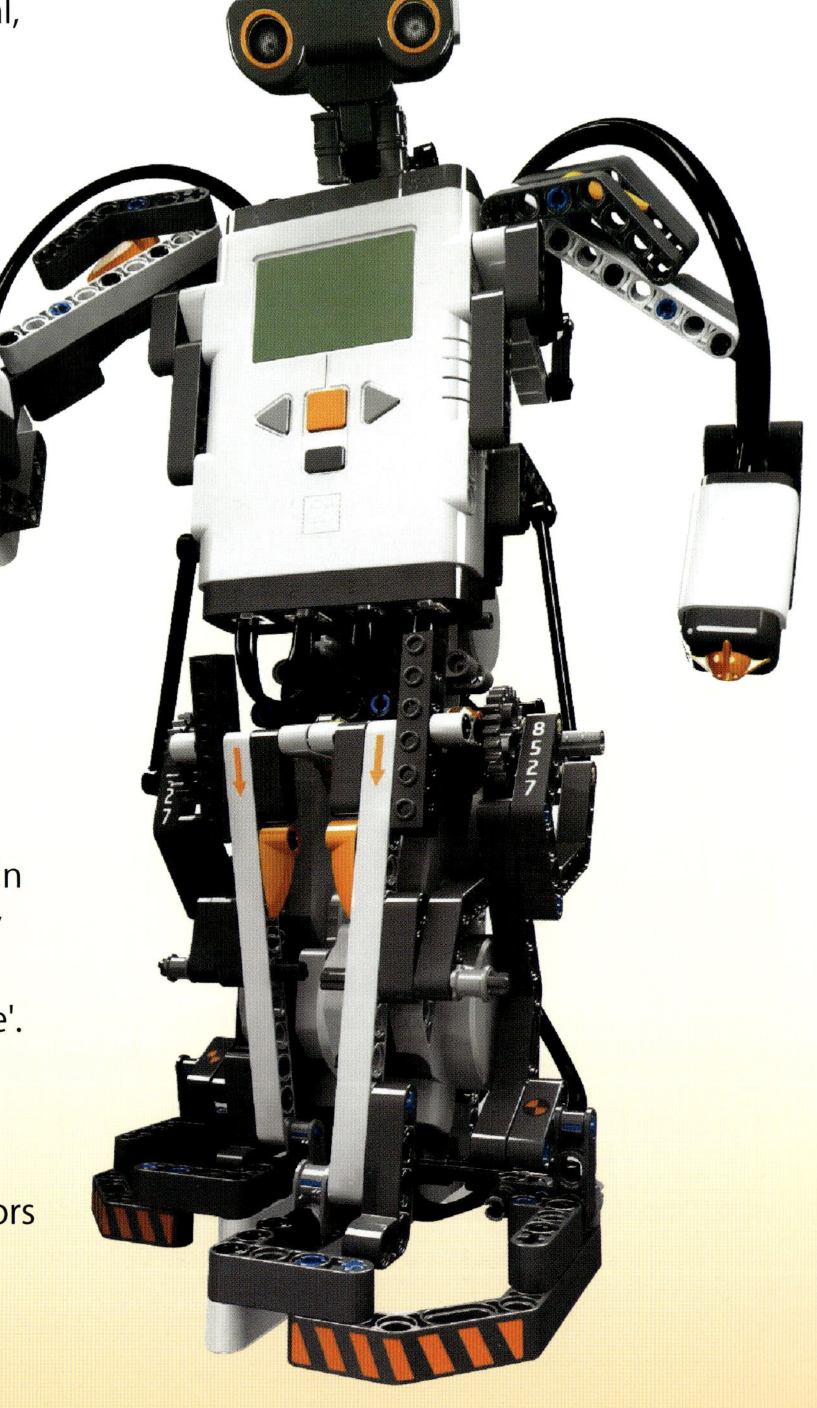

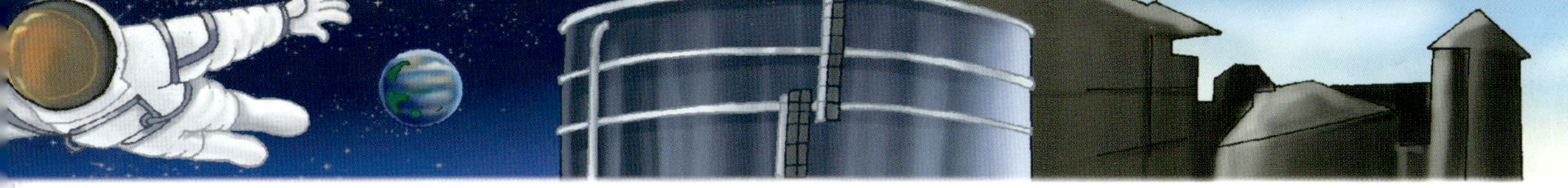

# Artificial limb

A limb or joint lost through accident, disease or birth defect maybe replaced with an artificial limb or joint. Such a replacement is called **prosthesis** from the Latin word meaning 'addition'. Crude artificial limbs have been used since the earliest loss of an arm, leg, hand or foot.

The modern era of artificial limbs began with the famous French surgeon Ambroise Pare (1517-1590; considered the 'father of modern surgery'). Pare began his career as a barber-surgeon. In 1536 he became a battlefield surgeon. On the battleground his greatest challenge was developing ways to deal with gunshot wounds. The devastating nature of these wounds meant that the soldiers' limbs often had to be amputated. After devising safer, more effective methods of amputation, Pare turned his attention to the design of artificial limbs to replace the ones he had surgically removed.

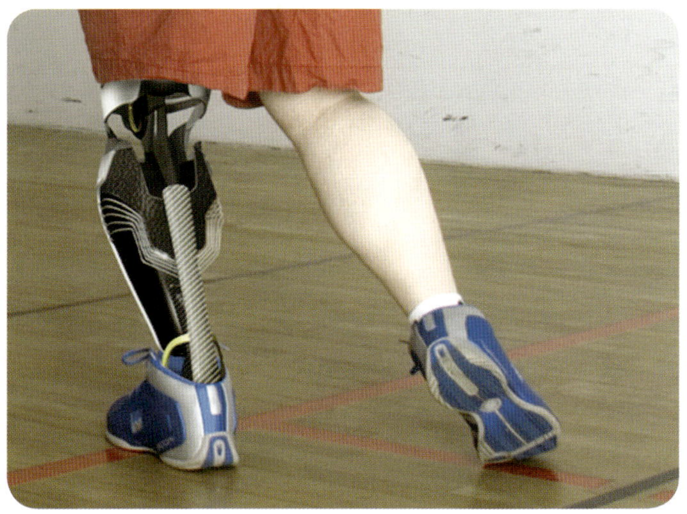

An artificial hand made by Pare had fingers that moved individually by means of tiny internal cogs and levers. When amputating a limb, Pare tried to leave enough stump so that it could be fitted with an artificial limb. Because of Pare's eminence, his ideas and designs for prostheses (plural of the word prosthesis) or artificial limbs became well-known.

Ambroise Pare

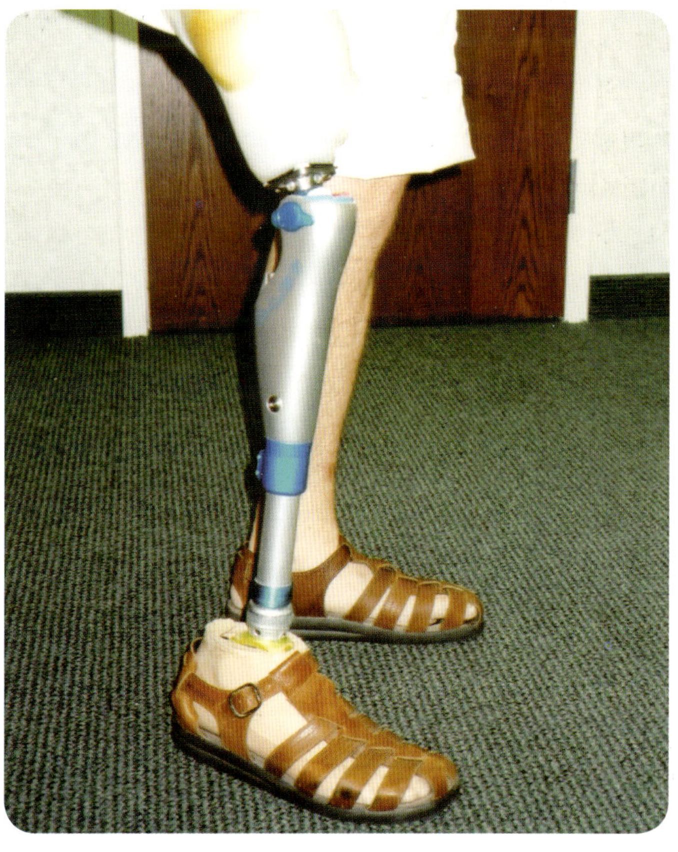

# The first vaccine—Smallpox vaccination

Edward Jenner

For many centuries, smallpox devastated mankind. In modern times we do not have to worry about it thanks to the remarkable work of Edward Jenner and later developments from his endeavours. In 1796, he invented the smallpox vaccination. Dr Jenner was aware of the belief that anybody who contracted cowpox, never contracted smallpox. He realized that inoculating people with cowpox would immunize them against smallpox. He researched this issue and performed a test to confirm his hypothesis. He inoculated an eight-year-old boy with matter taken from a cowpox pustule. The matter was taken from the hand of Sarah Nelmes, who had caught the disease from a cow named Blossom. Phipps developed coxpox and quickly recovered. Several weeks later, the boy was inoculated with smallpox, and did not contract the disease. And so, Dr Jenner created history and saved humanity from the deadly enemy called Smallpox.

**Karl Gothe Jansky was an American radio engineer who pioneered and developed radio astronomy. In 1932, he detected the first radio waves from a cosmic source —the central region of the Milky Way Galaxy.**

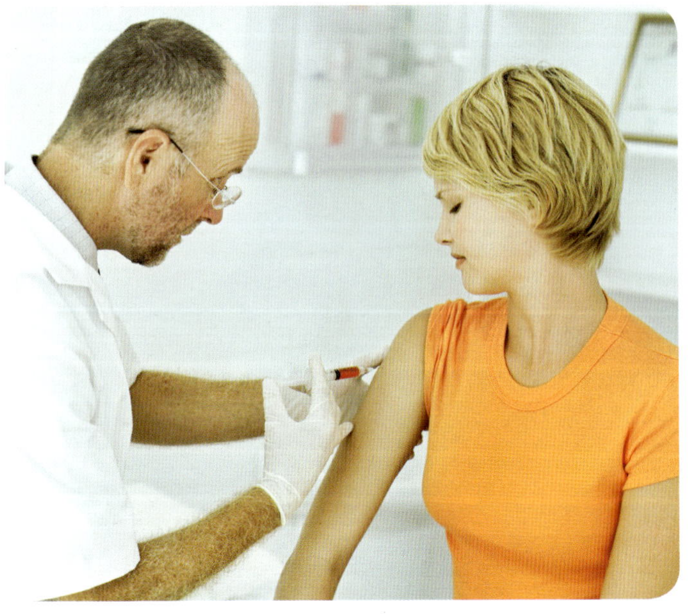

# Open-heart surgery

Opening the chest to operate directly on an exposed heart is major surgery. For many years the procedure was considered impossible because performing the operation would cause the heart to stop beating. A few pioneers, however, did perform emergency surgery directly on the open heart. One of the first was African-American surgeon Daniel Hale Williams. Williams opened the chest of a stabbed victim and sewed up the pericardium (the sac surrounding the heart) in 1893.

An American surgeon named John H. Gibbon Jr. devoted himself to solving this problem in the 1930s. Assisted by his wife Mary, Gibbon developed a workable pump-oxygenator in 1931. This heart-lung machine switched blood from the veins through a catheter (a slender tube) to a machine. The machine supplied the blood with oxygen and then pumped the blood back into the arteries. In 1953, Gibbon ushered in the era of open-heart surgery by using his heart-lung machine on a patient suffering from heart failure.

Daniel Hale Williams

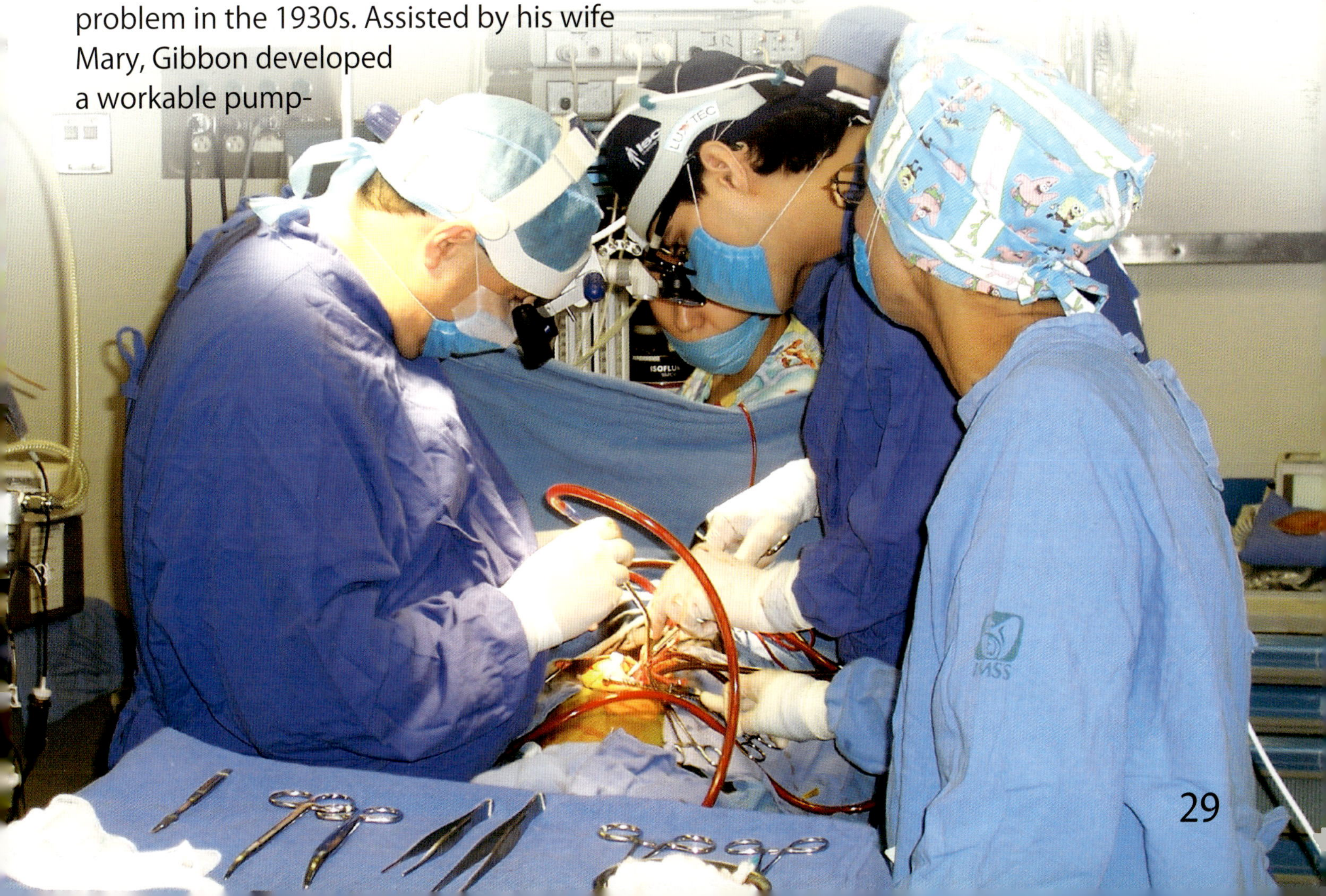

# The human genome

The genome consists of all the hereditary information of an organism. This information is passed through generations and is encoded by Deoxyribonucleic acid (DNA). The human genome is stored on 23 chromosome pairs. The one pair is sex-determining and remaining twenty two are autosomal chromosome pairs.

The Human Genome Project (HGP) was one of the great feats of exploration in history— an inward voyage of discovery rather than an outward exploration of the planet or the cosmos. It was an international research effort to sequence and map all of the human genes together, known as the human genome. Completed in April 2003, the HGP gave us the ability to, for the first time, to read nature's complete genetic blueprint for building a human being.

The HGP has revealed that the size of the human genome is about 109 base pairs and there are probably about 20,500 human genes. The completed human sequence can now identify their locations. This ultimate product of the HGP has given the world a resource of detailed information about the structure, organization and function of the complete set of human genes. This information can be thought of as the basic set of inheritable 'instructions' for the development and function of a human being.

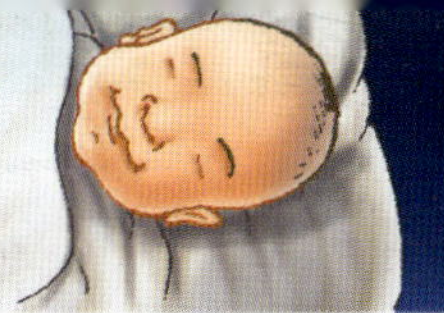
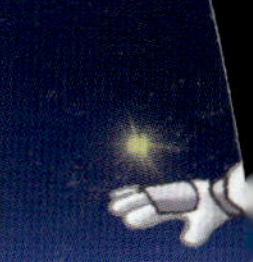

# Index

# Test Your MEMORY

1. Which spacecraft made the first safe landing on the moon?
2. When was the first motorbike invented?
3. How did the process of photography evolve?
4. When was the first photograph taken?
5. What was the ARPANET?
6. What is aspirin used for?
7. Who invented the first microscope?
8. When was the first animal cloned?
9. Name the first antibiotic drug.
10. Who invented the first robot?
11. Who did the first successful open heart surgery?
12. What is the size of human genome?